THE SHY GUY GUIDES

VOLUME 1: UNDERSTANDING SHYNESS

Copyright

Alon, Doron M.

The Shy Guy Guides: Volume 1: Understanding Shyness —1st ed

Printed in the USA

ISBN: 978-0692590126

Images used for Cover and content:

All Photos are from Fotolia.com

#57700737 - Man With Two Women © Kakigori Studio

#56465506 - Friends Together Happily © Kakigori Studio

#29870934 © Piumadaquila

#58314747 © ayelet_keshet

#59205913 © Igor Zakowski

Disclaimer:

By law, I need to add this statement.

This volume of "The Shy Guy Guides" is for educational purposes only and does not claim to prevent or cure any disease. The advice and methods in this book should not be construed as financial ,medical or psychological treatment. Please seek advice from a professional if you have serious financial, medical or psychological issues.

By purchasing , reading and or listening to this book, you understand that results are not guaranteed. In light of this, you understand that in the event that this book or audio does not work or causes harm in any area of your life, you agree that you do not hold Doron M. Alon, Numinosity Press Inc, its employees or affiliates liable for any damages you may experience or incur.

About The Shy Guy Guides Series

The whole goal of the Shy Guy Guide series is to provide concise and practical information on shyness and how to defeat it. Everything written in these guide is based on mountains of research and personal experience. You can expect only the most up-to-date information and the most effective techniques in every volume of the Shy Guy Guide Series. To learn more about the Shy Guy Guides Series, please visit www.theshyguyguides.com. We will be adding new information often.

Introduction

Shyness is tough, isn't it? It sure was for me.

It prevents you from truly enjoying the moment when you are in social situations . What's worse, is that people pick up on your shyness and often misinterpret it as being aloof or antisocial. Being labeled those things is horrible and downright insulting. If only you could get outside of yourself long enough to show them that it's not true. That's what this series will help you do.

Shyness is all pervasive ,you are certainly not alone in this world, even if you might think that you are. Some studies suggest that about half of people experience some form of shyness. That number is likely to grow due to technological advances. When I was a kid in the 70s and 80s you had to actually go outside and play, you actually had to go up to people. I know, weird right? Nowadays , social interaction can take place without the, well, social interaction. It's for this reason you will find people can say what they want online but will seldom do so in person. Sound familiar? But it doesn't have to be that way, despite technology, we still need to interact face-to-face. You can't date yourself, and, well, a blowup doll can't exactly give you the mental stimulation you need either. Your shyness must be dealt with. Until now, the shyness has dealt with you.

Now, please understand, I am not going to claim the road to getting rid of, or that controlling your shyness is going to be an easy one to travel. It wasn't for me, but then again, you will see why it was so hard for me in the next chapter. One thing I can tell you is that what you will learn in this series will certainly help you in getting it under control , that is, if you apply the concepts. Tackling Shyness is not the only thing you will learn from this series, you will also learn more about who you are as a person. Many of the techniques in this series will open other psychological pathways that can help you in other areas of your life as well. The journey to conquering shyness is really a quest to find yourself.

In this volume, we will discuss the broader aspects of shyness.

Chapter 1:

My Story

There are so many social and environmental factors that can make a person shy. I just happen to have some of the major ones. This makes me especially qualified to write this series because I know what it is like to have shyness interfere with pretty much all areas of life. I grew up in a dysfunctional family. No surprise there, almost all of us come from one. My father was a SUPER SOCIAL person. This guy was the kind of guy that could talk. Not in a sleazy kind of way, but as an entertainer. He was a ladies' man and even when he lost his looks and health, his charm and personality was still able to woo them. He was the exact opposite of what shy is. He gained energy and courage from being around people. He was never shy... I on the other hand...lived in his shadow. I was always shy and that disappointed my father. Growing up with a father like that was not easy. Whenever I would withdraw, he would get upset, he never understood me. He thought my interests were boring. I tend to be a person who lives and gains energy from ideas. A lot of us shys are like that. He never understood that. I am more like my mother in my temperament. I guess you could say I am a momma's boy :).

My father has since passed away and I am sure , if he were alive today he would be proud to see how far I have come as it pertains to my social life.

I have been shy and introverted for most of my life. Almost all my activities were done alone when I was a kid. Although I had friends, I always preferred my own company. In that way, I am introverted. It is not to say that I didn't like socializing, I just liked alone time more. On the surface, that doesn't sound like much of a problem. Introversion is not shyness, it's a personality trait. However, I am also shy. When coupled with introversion it can lead to a heightened sense of shyness. A sense of shyness that mingles so seamlessly with the introverted personality that it morphs into a perfect storm of social anxiety, perceived aloofness and isolation. It got so bad for me that that I started abusing alcohol in order to relax myself before I went on dates or to large social gatherings, hell, even small gatherings. After awhile, the alcohol became a problem for me. I got so wrapped up that I ended up drinking even when not in a social setting.

You see, an introverted person needs to be in their own space in order to recharge their batteries. The shy person has approach anxiety and often times self esteem issues. Shyness strikes both the introverts and the extroverts. I have seen type A personalities cower away from asking someone on a date. That's shyness.

So for an introvert like me that needed to relax in my own space, that shyness caused so much anxiety my introverted nature kicked in often. I needed more and more time on my own to recover from the stress of shyness. Shyness is taxing on the mind and the first instinct for the introvert is to go into himself to recover. You see? it creates a vicious cycle. A cycle that takes normal shyness and introversion and melds them into a monstrous beast that gets only worse with time if it is not stopped in its tracks. I created such a beast in my own life and it nearly ate me alive. As I got older, my shyness got worse and worse. I slowed down my dating life, almost to a complete halt. In fact, It slowed down so much I didn't have sex for a few years and didn't have a real relationship in over 5. When I finally met someone, I felt almost as if I have never dated in my life. When I told her I didn't have sex in years nor a real long term relationship in 5, she looked at me as if I had a horn on my head. Well, suffice it to say, all my insecurities boiled over, and the drinking got worse. Eventually the relationship was over. That crushed me. One of the reasons she broke up with me was because I didn't take chances in life and I was too shy to meet her friends... Lesson learned.

It was only then that I decided it was time for me to change my life. Not just my social life but my entire life. From my finances to my fitness. Every since then, I have written over 20 books and a few have hit bestseller status. I got out of debt, lost 20 pounds and finally got the drinking under control. But in order to do that, I had to change my thinking, I needed to take more risks. The only way I was to change, was to stop letting my shyness hold me back from happiness. Remember, Shyness doesn't only affect your love life, it keeps you timid in almost all social situations, even if you are not actively in a social setting. For example, you might be shy at the gym in fear that people will judge you. Trust me, they aren't, they couldn't give a shit whether you lift 3 pounds or 300. You see? You might be too shy to start a business because you would need to interact with people. You might be too shy to ask your boss for a raise etc etc. It touches all areas where other people are involved. So, I had enough and decided to turn it all around.

In this series, I'll explain to you exactly how I did it. You won't find BS pickup lines or "get laid" techniques and strategies. You are going to learn about YOURSELF. You are going to learn that shyness doesn't need to hold you back anymore. You'll always feel a tad shy, some shyness is natural; but it doesn't have to stop you from living. When you take back what shyness has robbed from you, everything in your life will change... You'll see.

Doron

Chapter 2:

What Is Shyness?

There is one thing shyness isn't and that is introversion. They are completely different. As I stated in the previous chapter, introversion is a kind of personality trait. A trait Carl Jung coined to describe people who, unlike extroverts, need time to recuperate in their own space and gain energy from that space; they enjoy being in their mind and do not need as much outside stimulation. An introvert, however, once fully charged can be very social. So please do not get these two confused. Although both can be found together, one CAN be mutually exclusive of the other. This is very important to keep in mind. I will get deeper into that in the next chapter.

Shyness is also not social anxiety. Although they are very much related, social anxiety is a much broader category and often involves depressive states as well. Social anxiety can also induce panic attacks which is not often seen in simple shyness. In the end, only a trained psychological can determine the difference in a person. If you suspect you have a social anxiety disorder, you can still benefit from this series, BUT you should probably consult with a doctor as well. I am not a doctor and do not claim to be one.

Shyness is an internal state , a feeling of timidity, lack of assertiveness and apprehensiveness. These often irrational states are due to the misperceived notion that people will judge you, your actions or what you say or how you look. This fear, which is often unfounded eventually causes you to withdraw from people. You fear being criticized, you fear rejection and so you just withdraw so as not to place yourself in a situation that opens you up to those negative situations. It just seems easier to withdraw from the world than to engage in and with it.

This withdrawal has a few downsides. It removes you from enjoying your life. Avoiding POTENTIALLY painful situations is not the same as ENJOYING life. After awhile this withdrawal can inhibit your social skills. Trust me, I know all about that.

There are several potential causes to shyness. Some believe that it might be genetic. Although there is some evidence for this, it still , however, remains an hypothesis. Nothing has been proven genetically as of yet. The biggest determinant of shyness by far is your environment. It can stem from not being heard as a child, to more extreme cases as child abuse. It can also emerge suddenly from a very fearful situation. A situation that confers instant need to withdrawal from the world. Or , like me, you may have a parent that misunderstands you. I know for myself, I was shy first and then that shyness caused anxiety which brought me to drinking.

Shyness in some people can fade with time, however, I find that more often than not, a person needs to work through the shyness in order to overcome it.

Broad Symptoms Of Shyness:

Shyness, like so many other human behaviors can be seen and experienced on a wide spectrum. Some people have it worse than others. Symptoms can be rather benign like not knowing what to say. On the other hand, it can lead to physical symptoms that can be quite pronounced like shaking, rapid heartbeat, sweating. Other symptoms like not smiling and not establishing eye contact is also very common. This produces so much discomfort that a person will withdraw, which then creates a spiral of negative thoughts like " I am such a boring person" " What's wrong with me?" " I am not good enough"" I am such a loser"...Sound familiar? It sure does for me, when I was in the midst of my shyness I could barely muster up a smile. In one situation I was so shy that I left a social gathering without even saying goodbye to the host. I was like " Fuck it, I am outta here". YIKES!!! What was worse for me is that the host of this gathering was a beautiful , smart woman that I KNEW liked me back. Well, as you may have guessed, I never got a chance to date her. I ruined that because of my shyness. I recall calling a friend after I left and cried and cried and cried. I was so distraught about it. **As you probably know, shyness can be very debilitating**.

Here is a useful chart showing more detail symptoms of shyness. This chart can be found at:

http://www.shyness.com/encyclopedia.html

Behavior	Physiological	Cognitive	Affective
Inhibition and passivity	Accelerated heart rate	Negative thoughts about the self, the situation, and others	Embarrassment and painful self-consciousness
Gaze aversion	Dry mouth	Fear of negative evaluation and looking foolish to others	Shame
Avoidance of feared situations	Trembling or shaking	Worry and rumination, perfectionism	Low self-esteem
Low speaking voice	Sweating	Self-blaming attributions, particularly after social interactions	Dejection and sadness
Little body movement or expression or Excessive	Feeling faint or dizzy, butterflies in stomach or	Negative beliefs about the self (weak) and others	Loneliness

nodding or smiling	nausea	(powerful), often out of awareness	
Speech dysfluencies	Experiencing the situation or oneself as unreal or removed	Negative biases in the self-concept, e.g., "I am socially inadequate, unlovable, unattractive."	Depression
Nervous behaviors, such as touching one's hair or face	Fear of losing control, going crazy, or having a heart attack	A belief that there is a "correct" protocol that the shy person must guess, rather than mutual definitions of social situations	Anxiety

http://www.shyness.com/encyclopedia.html

Different Types of Shyness:

As I mentioned earlier, shyness might express itself in different ways in different people. This is very important to keep in mind. Not all shy people are experience the same thing. Broadly speaking, there are 2 types of shyness. There are , of course more complex subdivisions within each type.

1. The Socially Anxious Shy Person: I was certainly in this category of shyness. The symptoms of this kind of shyness is intense and excessive self consciousness and self preoccupation. In this shyness there is a preoccupation with how you look, what people are thinking of you etc. This is quite debilitating at times because you are constantly reading people's minds, thinking you know what they think about you. It's quite a tough thing to go through.

2. Publically Shy Person: I can also say that this shyness was also something I suffered. Talk about a double whammy. In this kind of shyness , we are most self conscious about what we say. Are we being awkward? Behaving oddly? Are we too quiet? Or too loud? In this form of shyness we often have a hard time giving and taking compliments. Don't I know it, I couldn't take a compliment no matter what.

Now that we have an idea of what Shyness is, let's get a bit deeper into the misconception that Shyness and Introversion are the same thing. It's important to get deeper into that and debunk that right off the bat.

Chapter 3:

Introversion vs. Shyness

I think it is very important to make the distinction between introversion and Shyness. Often times they are considered the same, but as I stated earlier, they are not the same, even if they appear to be superficially so.

This distinction for me was illuminating. When I realized that all my symptoms were actually symptoms of shyness and NOT introversion, it made the process of change take on a new dimension. Although I am introverted, the pain I felt was , in fact, shyness. I was under the false assumption that this painfully awkward and shy behavior I felt and exhibited was simply who I was as a person. It was only after I realized that who I Was and what I was feeling in social situations were not the same.

There is one HUGE distinction between introversion and shyness that not many people realize. Shyness produces pain, introversion generally does not. You don't choose to be shy in a situation, it is almost automatic, you feel that fear, that timidity, that intimidation. That causes you to enter a fight-or flight mode and you do everything you can to avoid it. You run away from social situations and avoid them all together, not by choice but from fear.

Introverts on the other hand do not feel a tremendous amount of discomfort in social situations. That fear you feel as a shy person is not always present in classic introversion. An introvert voluntarily reacts, whereas a shy person does not. An introvert is acting more by choice, not by fear. An introvert chooses to avoid or stay away from social situations not because they fear them, but because they simply get more joy in being alone. A shy person avoids them out of fear. It's the lack of discomfort and the exercising of choice that makes introversion and shyness so different. The desire for a quieter atmosphere (Introversion) and the fear of judgment (Shyness) are starkly different.

Although we now know the distinction, it doesn't mean others do and that can lead to both the introvert and the shy person to experience low self confidence. We will discuss that in the next chapter.

Chapter 4:

Societal views of Shyness

Different societies view sociability in different ways . These differing ways can determine whether a person feels good about being shy or not. Some collectivist cultures encourage shyness, shyness is a very positive trait to have in a culture that prides itself on being part of a group and the exercising of self control. It's for this reason the prototype of outgoingness; "Type-A" often have trouble making a good impression in other countries where the alpha-male personality is not considered an asset. In collectivist societies the shy person may not develop any negative feeling about his shyness.

Shy people, in general, are perceived quite negatively in western society. Western society places a high premium on sociability. It is for this reason a large part of the interview process to get a job is determined on your sociability. Often the person conducting the interview will not quite understand nor care if you are an introvert or just shy. If you appear shy, you're not likely to get the job. You are considered as " Not A Good Fit". Of course, it also depends upon the type of job you are going for. A job in a stockroom is not the same as a store greeter.

Because the western culture emphasizes super sociability , often times this can make a shy person withdraw even further and feel misunderstood. And you know what? The shy person is misunderstood. After awhile, the withdrawal creates an atmosphere which prevents the shy person from developing the needed social skills to live in an increasingly sociable society, as I stated earlier. Low self esteem is easily developed in a shy person in western societies since he will most likely be misunderstood as being aloof, arrogant and distant, this causes peers to reject that him. It's very painful to have such labels placed on you. I should know, I was called worse things than that. My father once called me a "Lemon" and that I would never achieve anything in life because I didn't portray outgoing characteristics. Another disturbing fact about western cultures view of shyness is how the medical field views it. When the cultural norm is the "Type A" personalities, the mental health fields start creating a structure that will deem anything other than sociable as a dysfunction or a personality disorder which further stigmatizes the shy person.

Being someone who grew up here in NYC, the home of Type-A, I know how hard it is to fit in when you are shy. It is a challenge, but let me tell you this. If you can conquer your shyness you will be able to do almost anything. Make it a personal goal and you will see just how great it can be to be more sociable. You don't need to agree with the western norm, but if you live in a western country that values sociability, you will need to adapt if you want to live a functional life. I know it might not always seem fair, but as they say, "No man is an island."

Chapter 5:

<u>The Positives and Negatives To Being Shy</u>

<u>The Positives</u>

There are benefits to being shy by the way. I know it might seem hard to imagine, but it is true.

- I found that not only with myself, but with other shy people , we tend to have deeper and more enduring friendships. I am 40 years old and I have a friend since kindergarten. All my friends are lifelong friends. That's because as shy people, we tend to have deeper connections to the friends we have. God knows it isn't easy for a shy person to make friends in the first place. We appreciate the ones we have. Another interesting thing to note is that , amongst friends, we are super social. Which is indication is that comfort level really determines how social we are.

- Shy people excel at work that requires independence. I know that's how it was for me. Although I have conquered my social shyness, I still have shy tendencies that help me in my life. Remember, just because you conquer shyness doesn't mean you are not still able to benefit from a shy tendency. You are still the same person, but less shy.

- We as shy people tend to enjoy things on a deeper level. When we are having fun, we are truly having fun. We appreciate it more. I know that sounds odd, but brain research suggest that people with a shy temperament have high sensitivity to both negative and positive experiences, much more than the average person.

- We as shy people tend to be in our heads a lot. In terms of social life, that is not so good. But it also carries over into other areas of our lives. We are often a " think before you act" kind of person. This can come in very handy in many aspects of life.

- Shy people are also good listeners, since we aren't blowing our own horns, we tend to have what it takes to listen closely to what others are saying.

These are all wonderful things and we will always possess them , even if we conquer shyness, its only when shyness takes control that shyness can start negatively impacting us. If you bought this book or any other books in this series, it might be the case for you.

The Negatives

As I mentioned in a previous chapter, depending where you are, shyness can be a liability. Since I am writing this book in a western culture, I will talk about the negatives from a western perspective. Since the western culture dominates much of the world, we need to learn how to manage within it.

- In western culture, as I stated earlier, places a higher premium on high social ability. More often than not, the shy person will not be in the CEO position; but a more gregarious fellow will be. Us shy folk tend to be the ones behind the scenes. I know this all too well, in every job I had with the exception of one, I was way behind the scenes or asked to be behind the scenes.

- Shyness , since it is an inhibiting behavior, it tends to keep us from experiencing new things in life. This is very painful. As life passes, shy people tend to stay stuck. It took me nearly 40 years to come to terms with my shyness. I am only truly living now. 20 years ago, if I knew what I know now, life would have been so different. Shyness robbed me of most of my life. **We can't let that happen to you.**

- Shy people also tend to be taken advantage of in western culture. Since we can't say no as easily as others, people think they can dump more of their work on us. You see, for the most part, they are not being mean by giving us more work. It's that the shy person doesn't speak up for himself so they think you are okay with more work. Don't expect others to read your mind. This is another thing I had to learn the hard way.

- Since shy people tend to shy away from social situations, loneliness can be a huge problem. Certainly not conducive to a healthy life. I have lived a lonely existence for most of my life. So I know how it feels. Loneliness has been proven to harm the health and longevity of a person. So in a very real sense, **Shyness can kill**.

- Shyness is also associated with alcohol and drug abuse. As I stated in chapter 1, that's what it did to me. Drinking started off as a social lubricant and then morphed into full-blown raging alcoholism. Drink made me feel less self conscious. It nearly ruined my entire life in the process. Learn from my mistake. Drinking and drugs will only place a Band-Aid on your shyness. In the end, once the drugs and alcohol become a habit, the shyness will actually increase and get worse. I thought I was shy before I started to drink, I became even more so after the ill effects of alcohol started to take over all aspects of my life. I isolated like you wouldn't believe. Take heed, it will only make shyness worse and harder to conquer. I blame the self medication with Alcohol as the # 1 reason I did not change my life sooner. Ill emphasize again, Don't make my mistake with drugging and drinking. I lost control and what turned out as a simple drink to relax became an addiction and it took me a very long time to get a handle on it.

- Although living in our heads is an asset at time, in most other times it is not. We tend to waste copious amount of time deciding whether or not interact in social situations.

- Sexual issue 1: Being able to, well, get it up can be harder for shy men because of performance anxiety. This anxiety is self fulfilling and quite painful mentally. It can be crushing for a man. This is also something I found out the hard way...no pun intended.

- Sexual issue 2: A study was done involving prostitutes and the kinds of men they picked up. Astonishingly, many more of the prostitutes clients were shy men who had difficulty communicating their sexual desires with wives and girlfriends. With a prostitute , a shy man stands a much better chance of NOT being rejected. That's what the shy man is trying to avoid, **Rejection**. Do you see how this can be problematic in life? This kind of risky behavior opens up a lot of dangers. Diseases being by far one of the worst. Luckily, I never resorted to this.

As you can see, in this culture, shyness is not an asset in the broad sense. Oddly enough, our obsession with technology, in many ways encourages shyness. Its one of those paradoxes. Western World is Type A, but encourages technology that encourages anything but Type A behavior. In the next chapter, we will discuss this in more depth.

Chapter 6

Does Technology Encourage Shyness?

Let me tell you a quick story: Online dating has always been ideal for me, I can talk to many women at once and do not really need to face them unless I really want to. There were times during the height of my shyness that I would speak to women. Later I would feel the pressure of meeting them and then suddenly shut down my dating profile because I was too shy to meet and too scared to tell the truth that I was not ready. How messed up is that? I would be so nervous about meeting that I literally turned those people off with a click of my mouse. See how easy technology made it for me to nurture my fear? Take heed.

With the advent of the internet, all sorts of forums and sites are created to foster communication. The landscape of interpersonal communication has changed so rapidly, it's quite amazing actually. Ironically, the more connected we are to each other technologically, the less face-to face interaction there is. We are more social but in a paradoxically antisocial way. Think about it, how often are you in front of people other than work and maybe grocery shopping? Do you do your banking online? Shopping online? When you speak to friends and family are you calling them? Seeing them face to face? Or emailing / texting them? See what I mean? We are being social in very unsocial ways. One could say , well, times are changing, it's a new paradigm. Yes, this is true and please do not misunderstand me. I am a technology junkie so I am not condemning it. I am just saying that if you pay close attention, technology is fostering the very behavior you want to correct. Technology allows you to hide behind a screen.

Once upon a time, the work environment was probably the most social a person would get in their day to day lives. Nowadays, everyone is emailing everyone else. You only see a few sporadic face-to-faces.

Now, on the outset, as a shy person you may feel pretty good about all this. That means fewer and fewer opportunities for you to feel uncomfortable. Well, on the outset that is correct. However, the lack of situations where face-to-face encounters are required put us at a steep disadvantage long term. Since we never have an opportunity to be social, we never develop the courage or the skills to be. Remember, fighting shyness is not only about being shy, it is also about developing life skills in general. Do you see how this can be a problem? If you are never exposed to the stimuli you need for change, you will never change. It's like going to the gym, if you want to gain muscle **YOU HAVE TO GO TO THE GYM**. You must be in situation that fosters that kind of stimuli. So in order to break this technology trap, we must do more things to get out of the trap and get out there. In upcoming volumes of the The Shy Guy Series, I will give you exact methods of doing so.

Now it is not all doom and gloom in regards to technology. It's through technology that we can also become less shy, but only if we use the technology as a tool and not for the interaction itself. We use it to make the initial connection and then we go out there and meet. In this way, technology is not a hiding place but a transportation vehicle to the public square.

So please take heed of technology, it is very good, but it can also stifle you. As I mentioned earlier, you will learn how to slowly ease out of hiding and into the real world. As painful as it to hear this, the internet is not the real world, it is only a window into it. Just like the window in your room, you can see the world outside, but the window itself is not the outside world.

Chapter 7

What's next?

As I stated in the introduction , this volume dealt with the broader aspects of what shyness is. In the upcoming volumes of this series, we will discuss the following:

Volume 2: Building a Solid Foundation Against Shyness

How Your Mind Works and Lies you tell yourself:

As John Milton stated " The Mind is its own place, it can make a heaven of hell, a hell of heaven" You will learn aspects of your mind that you may not have realized before. The mind is adept at telling us lies that hijack our lives. Often times we don't even know it is doing so. Its done out of maliciousnesss, but rather for our survival against a threat that doesn't really exist. We discuss this in volume 2.

How to deal with anxiety:

Anxiety is at the core of shyness, we will go through various steps that will help you deal with anxiety. It will not just be techniques that quiet the mind, but also common sense strategies that can shift your thinking patterns.

The Inner Traps of Social Anxiety:

You will learn how social anxiety creates a trap that is self perpetuating. Ill show you how not to fall into it.

Retake Control of your mental state and deal with bad mental habits:

Like any habit, the more you do it , the stronger it becomes. Shyness is no different. Shyness like other modes of thinking and behaving are very much habits and thus need to be handled as such. You will learn how to deal with various bad mental habits that foster shyness.

How to Strengthen your self confidence:

You will learn methods to improving yourself confidence. Lack of confidence and shyness are intimately related. Shyness is a lack of self confidence at its core.

Building Mental Resilience:

You will learn techniques to keep your mind resilient to stress and other pressures. A resilient mind is the best antidote to shyness.

Mindfulness - Stepping Back:

You will learn mindfulness techniques that will help you focus your mind and slowly but surely defeat your shyness. This is not just some meditation, it involves 2 other modalities that you might not be aware of. They may seem silly at first, but they work like a charm...Stay tuned.

Volume 3: Building a Solid Social Network

The Importance of A Strong Social Network:

Despite being inclined to shyness, I will get into some detail as to why it is of vital importance for you to build a strong social network. Remember, **No man is an island.**

Body Language and Eye contact:

As shys, we generally have a hard time hiding our discomfort and seldom give sustained eye contact. You will learn about developing confident body language and real, sustained eye contact. Both very important to beating shyness. As they say, change your body and the mind will follow.

Developing Good Conversation Skills:

Another tough thing we as shys encounter, we are notoriously berating ourselves about our conversation skills. You will learn the fundamentals of good communications skills. Oh and, our shyness can actually help us with this.

How to defeat "Approach Anxiety" in Social situations without fear of rejection:

You will learn how to defeat approach anxiety without having a heart attack :)

Ways to Make More Friends who have common Interest as you:

Since we tend to have a hard time making friends because we shy away from social situations, in this part of the series you will learn how to leverage technology instead of hiding behind it.

Advanced Techniques to Enhance Charisma:

We will discuss advanced and novel techniques that will help you develop your charisma, Warning, please keep an open mind :)

The Desire For Companionship is Innate:

Whether we fear companionship or not, the fact is, we are all hardwired to crave it. When you understand this, you will realize that wanting it and going for it is okay and that YOU CAN get the love that you want.

She might be beautiful, but is she good for you?

If you are like most guys, the sight of a beautiful woman does something to you. And I don't just mean getting you horny . It's like looking at an angel. Do you know what I mean? We suddenly feel the great desire to have her draped on our arm. Ohhhh what a wonderful feeling. Well, let me tell you this, if you base your choice of women solely on looks, watch out, you can get burned hard. Sure, attraction matters, but having the most beautiful woman in the room may not be all that its cracked up to be. I'll explain more in volume 4 of this series.

Why The LunkHeads get the girls:

Do you ever notice sometimes that a guy that has no looks or brains gets the woman you want? Why do you think that is? Ill explain that as well.

How to rid yourself of Relationship killing Behaviors:

As shys, we have an arsenal of behaviors and mental habits that are not conducive to holding down a relationship, in this book, I'll explain what they are and how to conquer them.

Dealing With Anxiety When you Approach women:

Dealing with anxiety when you approach women is all in the mind. I'll explain. Hint: She can't do anything to harm you. Only you have control over whether you get harmed.

How to come off without appearing Needy:

Although we might be shy, we still crave human interaction. Whether it be from friends or a lover. When enough time passes, we become emotional deserts, thirsting so much for that interaction. That thirst can often lead us to act needy, even when we don't want to. I know this from firsthand experience. I'll show you how to stop that from happening.

How to take rejection and make it empowering:

Probably one of the most important Chapters in volume 4. We will discuss how to turn rejection into personal power. YES, it can be done.

Visit www.theshyguyguides.com and sign up for our newsletter. Be informed as to when new volumes are coming out. You won't want to miss them.

Conclusion

There you have it, this volume was a quick overview of what shyness is and the positive and negative aspects of shyness in general. The subsequent volumes will be substantially longer since they are the meat of the series.

I want to thank you again for buying this book. Check out theshyguyguides.com and join our mailing list to find out when new volumes will be published **(Hint: By mid-July 2016, if not sooner.)** and other tools that can help you conquer shyness will be added as well.

About The Author

Doron Alon is a former shy guy and bestselling author of 50 books in 5 genres and is founder of Numinosity Press Inc.

He writes on a wide variety of topics including History, Self-help, Self-Publishing, Psychology and Spirituality. Doron's background and 24 years of experience in meditation training, Meridian tapping (also known as E.F.T), Subliminal Messaging and other modalities has made him a much sought after expert in the self help and spiritual fields. His conversational writing style and his ability to take complex topics and make them easily accessible has gained him popularity in the genres that he writes for.

To learn more about his other books on a wide variety of topics please visit www.doronalon.com or visit his author pages below on amazon.com

If you have any questions, please feel free to email him at doron@numinositypress.com

Doron's Author Pages:

History: https://www.amazon.com/author/dmalon

Spirituality: http://www.amazon.com/author/doronalon

Self Publishing: https://www.amazon.com/author/dalon

Bibliography:

http://news.sciencemag.org/2006/06/rewards-being-shy

http://www.ius.edu/shyness/

Shyness: How Normal Behavior Became a Sickness - Christopher Lane

Overcome Social Anxiety and Shyness - Beau Norton

Shyness: Understanding, Hope and Healing - Bernardo J. Carducci

http://www.shyness.com/encyclopedia.html

www.ingramcontent.com/pod-product-compliance
Lightning Source LLC
Chambersburg PA
CBHW071939020426
42331CB00010B/2934

9 780692 590126